Piano • Vocal • Guitar

The Oscar Hammerstein II
COLLECTION

Williamson Music would like to thank the family of Oscar Hammerstein II for the

photos, stories and memories they shared in the creation of this collection.

ISBN 0-7935-5034-3

WILLIAMSON MUSIC®

A RODGERS AND HAMMERSTEIN COMPANY

EXCLUSIVELY DISTRIBUTED BY

HAL•LEONARD™ CORPORATION

7777 W. BLUEMOUND RD. P.O. BOX 13819 MILWAUKEE, WI 53213

CONTENTS

1

2

3

Introduction
by William Hammerstein

Johnny Mercer said it best: "Accentuate the positive." That was what my father, Oscar Hammerstein II, spent his life writing songs about. He knew that the world was filled with many unpleasant things and ideas and people, but he was devoted to expressing the good things, the *positive* ideas and the *nicest* people. Once he said, "You wouldn't describe a tree only as it looks in winter."

I invite you to read his lyrics with attention to the moods and attitudes they tell us about. You'll discover that with all the wonderful songs celebrating love and beauty and optimism (like "Oh What A Beautiful Mornin'," "Hello, Young

Lovers," "Make Believe," and "A Cock-Eyed Optimist"), he also wrote songs of melancholy, ("It Might As Well Be Spring," "Love, Look Away"), sadness ("Lover, Come Back To Me") and anger ("You've Got To Be Carefully Taught") — not to mention irony ("Pore Jud Is Daid," "The Gentleman Is A Dope"), yearning ("Everybody's Got A Home But Me") and even despair ("Why Was I Born?").

How did he develop the talent and ability to express such varied feelings and points of view? Well, he grew up in the theatre; his father, Willy Hammerstein, managed a well-known and very successful Vaudeville House (Hammerstein's Victoria) built in New

York City's Times Square by *his* father, the first Oscar Hammerstein, about one hundred years ago. So Oscar II was exposed at a very young age to the kind of humor, some bawdy and cynical, that was a part of the texture of vaudeville. He learned sensitivity and compassion through his devotion to his mother, a beautiful Scottish girl who died when he was still young and left him with memories of love and tenderness. When he began his writing career he was fortunate to be tutored by Otto Harbach, a successful librettist and lyricist of the early years of this century. (In later life Oscar was gratified to return the favor by performing a similar role with young Stephen Sondheim.)

4

5

6

7

Living his life as a member of a busy and prominent theatrical family, he understood the theatre as a professional. He was proud to think of himself as a craftsman, although many have considered him an artist. He practiced his craft meticulously. It took him a long time and lots of work before he accepted the result. As I grew up in *his* home, I learned that the work was serious and one's attitude towards it reverent, even if the product sometimes seemed frivolous.

My siblings and I were brought up by him with love and strictness though, of course, as we grew older we decided that he had made mistakes that left us with problems. No, he was certainly not the perfect parent, but we were nevertheless grateful that he was ours. And in our later life we learned that whatever we felt had been errors in our up-bringing had to be corrected by us, and couldn't be blamed on him. Naturally, he covered that subject in the graduation scene in *Carousel.*

As for me, I'm happy and proud to be a member of this family, and grateful to have had him as my father. I am also immensely pleased to see the publication of this folio of his best work and hopeful all of you will enjoy the pleasure of exploring his use of words as much as he enjoyed putting them together in his inimitable way.

William Hammerstein
Washington, Connecticut
Autumn, 1995

PHOTO KEY

1-With daughter Alice; **2**-Halsman portrait of Oscar and Dorothy Hammerstein; **3**-With oldest son William; **4**-(From l. to r.) James Hammerstein, Dorothy Hammerstein, Nedda Logan, Oscar Hammerstein II and Stephen Sondheim (1946); **5**-Dorothy Hammerstein's sister Doodie and her family visit the Hammersteins at Highland Farm in Doylestown, Pennsylvania (1942); **6**-With step-daughter Susan; **7**-With Dorothy at Highland Farm.

Oscar Hammerstein II: Biography

Oscar Hammerstein II was born on July 12, 1895 in New York City. His father, William, was a theatre manager and for many years director of Hammerstein's Victoria, the most popular vaudeville theatre of its day. His uncle, Arthur Hammerstein, was a successful Broadway producer and his grandfather, Oscar Hammerstein, a famous opera impresario.

Hammerstein started writing lyrics for the Columbia University Varsity shows while studying law. His earliest works included musical comedies written with a Columbia undergraduate seven years his junior named Richard Rodgers. (The 1920 Varsity show, *Fly With Me*, was composed by Rodgers with lyrics by both Hammerstein and a fellow classmate of his named Lorenz Hart.) Withdrawing from Columbia Law School after his second year to pursue a career in theatre, Hammerstein took a job with his uncle as an assistant stage manager.

In 1919 Hammerstein's first play, *The Light*, was produced by his Uncle Arthur; it lasted four performances. Undaunted, he continued to write both lyrics and librettos, principally with Otto Harbach as his collaborating author. His first success, with Harbach, Vincent Youmans and Herbert Stothart, was *Wildflower* in 1923.

Hammerstein found his niche with some of the greatest composers of his day, breathing new life into the moribund artform of operetta with such classics as *Rose-Marie* (music by Rudolf Friml), *The Desert Song* (Sigmund Romberg,) *The New Moon* (Romberg,) and *Song Of The Flame* (George Gershwin.) With Jerome Kern, Hammerstein wrote eight musicals, including *Sweet Adeline*, *Music In The Air* and their master work, *Show Boat*. His last musical before embarking in an exclusive partnership with Richard Rodgers was *Carmen Jones*.

In 1943, Hammerstein, pioneer in the field of operetta, joined forces with Richard Rodgers who had, for

the previous twenty-five years, taken great strides in the field of musical comedy with his longtime partner, Lorenz Hart. The first Rodgers & Hammerstein collaboration, *Oklahoma!*, merged the two styles into a completely new genre — the musical play — and simultaneously launched the most successful partnership in the American musical theater. Over the next seventeen years Rodgers & Hammerstein wrote eight more Broadway musicals: *Carousel, Allegro, South Pacific, The King And I, Me And Juliet, Pipe Dream, Flower Drum Song* and *The Sound Of Music*. They also wrote a movie musical (*State Fair*) and one for television (*Cinderella*). Collectively their works have earned

26 Tony Awards, 14 Academy Awards, two Pulitzer Prizes and two Grammy Awards.

As producers, Rodgers & Hammerstein presented plays, musicals and revivals, including John van Druten's *I Remember Mama*, Anita Loos' *Happy Birthday*, Irving Berlin's blockbuster *Annie Get Your Gun*, the national tour of *Show Boat* (1947-49) and six of their stage musicals (from the Pulitzer winning *South Pacific* in 1949 to the Tony winning *The Sound Of Music* ten years later.) They also produced the motion picture of *Oklahoma!* and founded their own music publishing firm, Williamson Music (basing the name on the fact

that both of their fathers were named William.)

Oscar Hammerstein II was a member of the board of directors of many professional organizations, including the Dramatists Guild and the Screen Writers' Guild. He received many personal honors and awards including five honorary degrees, two Pulitzer Prizes, two Academy Awards, a special Grammy Award and five Tony Awards.

On August 23, 1960, Oscar Hammerstein II died at his farm in Doylestown, Pennsylvania. *The Sound Of Music* had been his last work for the theatre; "Edelweiss" was the last lyric he wrote.

1

2

3

Collaboration: The Biggest Word in the Theater

In the course of his career, Oscar Hammerstein II collaborated with nearly two dozen fellow lyricists, librettists and composers. In addition to his prolific partnerships with Jerome Kern (8 musicals) and Richard Rodgers (11 musicals), Hammerstein collaborated with, among others, Rudolf Friml, Sigmund Romberg, George Gershwin, Kurt Weill, Vincent Youmans and, posthumously, Georges Bizet. In the introduction to his compendium, Lyrics, *first published in 1949, Hammerstein discusses the importance of collaboration in the theater:*

Collaboration is the biggest word in the theater. It is the most important element in theatrical success. Not just the collaboration between an author and a composer, but the total collaboration in every play, the convergence and coordination of all the different talents, — producing, writing, directing, choreography, acting, scene designing, costume designing, lighting, orchestration, theater management, public relations — the mixture of all these ingredients is essential to every theatrical meal that seeks to make itself palatable to the public. To get along in the theater you must enjoy working side by side with other people. You must be willing not only to give your best to them but to accept their best and give them the opportunity of adding their efforts to yours to their full capacities.

One novelist recently stated that she was leaving the theater and returning to writing exclusively for the printed page. She said that she could not stand so many people advising her and helping her and butting in on her work. She did not like the feel of the director's hot breath on her neck. She was right to leave. If you want privacy in your work, and if you want to make your flights of fancy solo, stay away from the theater. The theater is a welding of many arts into one. No one person can be efficient or talented in all of these arts, and if any man could write and produce and direct and act and play the music, shift the scenery, design the costumes and, in short, do everything that could be done on one stage and come up with what was literally a one-man show, he would still need one more thing, an audience. You cannot get away from collaboration.

4

5

6

7

8

9

P H O T O   K E Y

1-With director Rouben Mamoulian during preparations for OKLAHOMA! (1943); **2**-With Joshua Logan and Richard Rodgers during rehearsals for SOUTH PACIFIC (1949); **3**-Writing MUSIC IN THE AIR with Jerome Kern (1932); **4**-Working on the score for THE KING AND I with Richard Rodgers (1951); **5**-With Julie Andrews and Richard Rodgers on the set of the television musical CINDERELLA (1957); **6**-With Florenz Ziegfeld and Jerome Kern during the run of SHOW BOAT (1927); **7**-With Sigmund Romberg (1931); **8**-On location for the movie version of OKLAHOMA! with director Fred Zinnemann (1954); **9**-With early collaborator Herbert Stothart (1920).

INDIAN LOVE CALL

from ROSE-MARIE (1924)

Lyrics by OTTO HARBACH and OSCAR HAMMERSTEIN II
Music by RUDOLF FRIML

12

WHO?

from SUNNY (1925)

Lyrics by OTTO HARBACH and OSCAR HAMMERSTEIN II
Music by JEROME KERN

THE DESERT SONG

from THE DESERT SONG (1926)

Lyrics by OTTO HARBACH and OSCAR HAMMERSTEIN II
Music by SIGMUND ROMBERG

CAN'T HELP LOVIN' DAT MAN

from SHOW BOAT (1927)

Lyrics by OSCAR HAMMERSTEIN II
Music by JEROME KERN

MAKE BELIEVE

from SHOW BOAT (1927)

Lyrics by OSCAR HAMMERSTEIN II
Music by JEROME KERN

The game of "just sup-pos-ing" is the sweet-est game I know,

Our dreams are more ro-man-tic than the world we see.

OL' MAN RIVER

from SHOW BOAT (1927)

Lyrics by OSCAR HAMMERSTEIN II
Music by JEROME KERN

Col-ored folks work on de Mis-sis-sip-pi, Col-ored folks work while de white folks play,

Pull-in' dose boats from de dawn to sun-set, Git-tin' no rest till de judge-ment day.

WHY DO I LOVE YOU?

from SHOW BOAT (1927)

Lyrics by OSCAR HAMMERSTEIN II
Music by JEROME KERN

I'm walk - ing on the air, dear, —— For life is

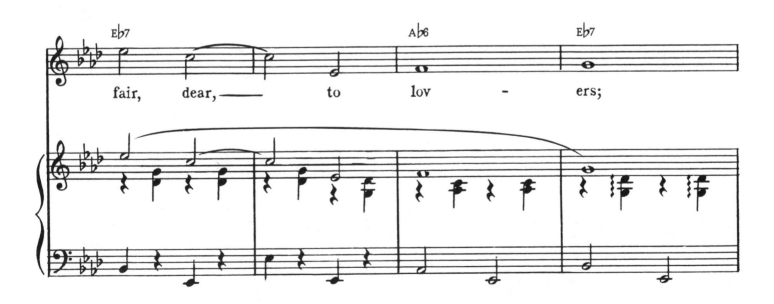

fair, dear, —— to lov - ers;

I'm in —— the sev – enth heav – en —— (There's more than

sev – en, —— my heart dis – cov – ers),

In this sweet, im – prob-a – ble and un – real world,

Find – ing you has giv-en me my i – deal world.

LOVER, COME BACK TO ME

from THE NEW MOON (1928)

Lyrics by OSCAR HAMMERSTEIN II
Music by SIGMUND ROMBERG

STOUTHEARTED MEN

from THE NEW MOON (1928)

Lyrics by OSCAR HAMMERSTEIN II
Music by SIGMUND ROMBERG

46

YOU ARE LOVE

from SHOW BOAT (1927)

Lyrics by OSCAR HAMMERSTEIN II
Music by JEROME KERN

48

Here's — a bright and beau-ti-ful world — all new Wrapped

up — in you. —

Tempo di Valse

Burthen

You — are love, here in my arms

Where you be - long, And here you will stay. I'll not let you a-

a piacere

way; I want day af-ter day with you.

You are spring, Bud of ro-mance un-furl'd, You taught me to see One truth for-ev-er true.

52

DON'T EVER LEAVE ME

from SWEET ADELINE (1929)

Lyrics by OSCAR HAMMERSTEIN II
Music by JEROME KERN

WHY WAS I BORN?

from SWEET ADELINE (1929)

Lyrics by OSCAR HAMMERSTEIN II
Music by JEROME KERN

I'VE TOLD EV'RY LITTLE STAR

from MUSIC IN THE AIR (1932)

Lyrics by OSCAR HAMMERSTEIN II
Music by JEROME KERN

THE SONG IS YOU

from MUSIC IN THE AIR (1932)

Lyrics by OSCAR HAMMERSTEIN II
Music by JEROME KERN

CAN I FORGET YOU

from HIGH, WIDE AND HANDSOME (1937, film)

Lyrics by OSCAR HAMMERSTEIN II
Music by JEROME KERN

Refrain (*slowly*)

THE FOLKS WHO LIVE ON THE HILL

from HIGH, WIDE AND HANDSOME (1937, film)

Lyrics by OSCAR HAMMERSTEIN II
Music by JEROME KERN

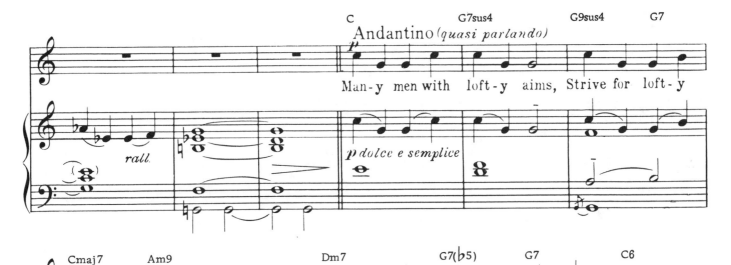

Man-y men with loft-y aims, Strive for loft-y

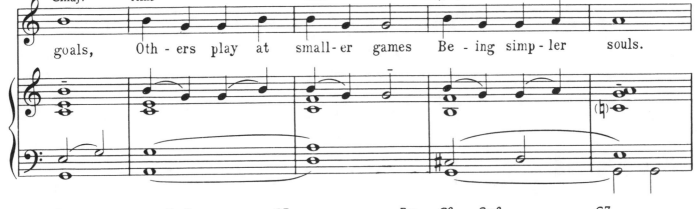

goals, Oth-ers play at small-er games Be-ing simp-ler souls.

I am of the lat-ter brand; All I want to do Is to find a spot of land,

72

"The folks who live on the hill!"

Some day we may be add-ing a thing or two,—

Note: The false accent is desired.

a wing or two,— We will make chang - es as an - y fam'-ly

will, But we will al - ways be called

ALL THE THINGS YOU ARE

from VERY WARM FOR MAY (1939)

Lyrics by OSCAR HAMMERSTEIN II
Music by JEROME KERN

Some day my hap-py arms will hold you, And some day I'll know that mo-ment di - vine, When all the things you are, are mine!

mine!

THE LAST TIME I SAW PARIS

from LADY, BE GOOD (1941)
from TILL THE CLOUDS ROLL BY (1946)

Lyrics by OSCAR HAMMERSTEIN II
Music by JEROME KERN

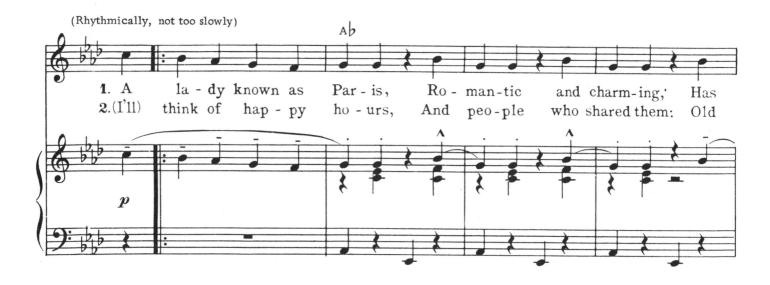

1. A la-dy known as Par-is, Ro-man-tic and charm-ing, Has
2. (I'll) think of hap-py ho-urs, And peo-ple who shared them: Old

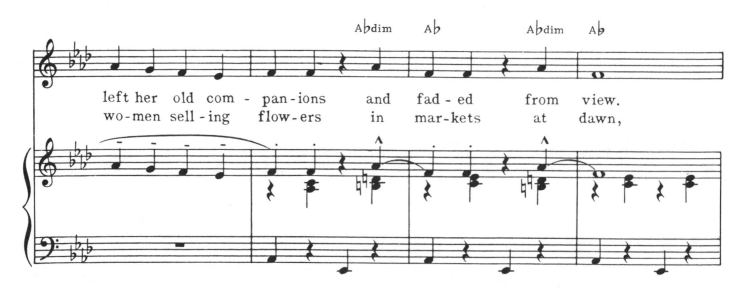

left her old com-pan-ions and fad-ed from view.
wo-men sell-ing flow-ers in mar-kets at dawn,

DAT'S LOVE

(Habanera)

from CARMEN JONES (1943)

Lyrics by OSCAR HAMMERSTEIN II
Music by GEORGES BIZET

I CAIN'T SAY NO!

from OKLAHOMA! (1943)

Lyrics by OSCAR HAMMERSTEIN II
Music by RICHARD RODGERS

91

KANSAS CITY

from OKLAHOMA! (1943)

Lyrics by OSCAR HAMMERSTEIN II
Music by RICHARD RODGERS

98

MANY A NEW DAY

from OKLAHOMA! (1943)

Lyrics by OSCAR HAMMERSTEIN II
Music by RICHARD RODGERS

Nev-er-'ve I wan-dered through the rye, won-der-ing where has some guy gone;

1. Man - y a new day will dawn be - fore I do!

2. dawn ___ Man - y a red sun will set! Man - y a blue moon will

shine be - fore I do!

OH, WHAT A BEAUTIFUL MORNIN'

from OKLAHOMA! (1943)

Lyrics by OSCAR HAMMERSTEIN II
Music by RICHARD RODGERS

OKLAHOMA

from OKLAHOMA! (1943)

Lyrics by OSCAR HAMMERSTEIN II
Music by RICHARD RODGERS

PORE JUD IS DAID

from OKLAHOMA! (1943)

Lyrics by OSCAR HAMMERSTEIN II
Music by RICHARD RODGERS

112

folks 'at real - ly knowed him, *knowed 'at beneath them two dirty shirts he always* wore, there beat a heart as big as all out - doors. As big as all out - doors. Jud Fry loved his fel - low man. He loved his fel - low man.

CURLY: (speaks)

He loved the birds of the forest and the beasts of the field. He loved the mice and the vermin in the barn, and he treated the rats like equals, which was right.

THE SURREY WITH THE FRINGE ON TOP

from OKLAHOMA! (1943)

Lyrics by OSCAR HAMMERSTEIN II
Music by RICHARD RODGERS

118

120

IF I LOVED YOU

from CAROUSEL (1945)

Lyrics by OSCAR HAMMERSTEIN II
Music by RICHARD RODGERS

124

IT MIGHT AS WELL BE SPRING

from STATE FAIR (1945, film)

Lyrics by OSCAR HAMMERSTEIN II
Music by RICHARD RODGERS

IT'S A GRAND NIGHT FOR SINGING

from STATE FAIR (1945, film)

Lyrics by OSCAR HAMMERSTEIN II
Music by RICHARD RODGERS

JUNE IS BUSTIN' OUT ALL OVER

from CAROUSEL (1945)

Lyrics by OSCAR HAMMERSTEIN II
Music by RICHARD RODGERS

REFRAIN

Fresh and a-live and gay and young, June is a love song sweet-ly sung__

June makes the bay look bright and new, Sails gleam-in' white on sun-lit blue.__

June!

June!

June!

WHEN THE CHILDREN ARE ASLEEP

from CAROUSEL (1945)

Lyrics by OSCAR HAMMERSTEIN II
Music by RICHARD RODGERS

142

YOU'LL NEVER WALK ALONE

from CAROUSEL (1945)

Lyrics by OSCAR HAMMERSTEIN II
Music by RICHARD RODGERS

ALL THROUGH THE DAY

from CENTENNIAL SUMMER (1946)

Lyrics by OSCAR HAMMERSTEIN II
Music by JEROME KERN

THE GENTLEMAN IS A DOPE

from ALLEGRO (1947)

Lyrics by OSCAR HAMMERSTEIN II
Music by RICHARD RODGERS

154

SO FAR

from ALLEGRO (1947)

Lyrics by OSCAR HAMMERSTEIN II
Music by RICHARD RODGERS

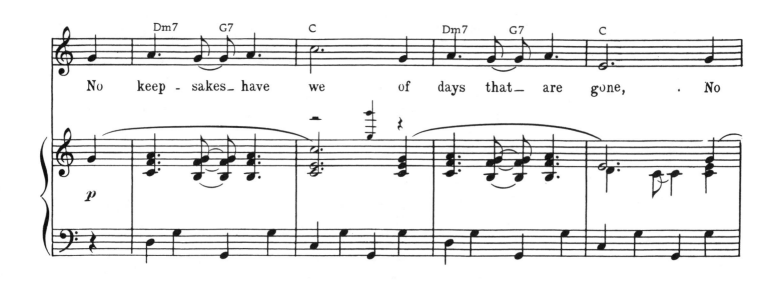

No keep - sakes_ have we of days that_ are gone, . No

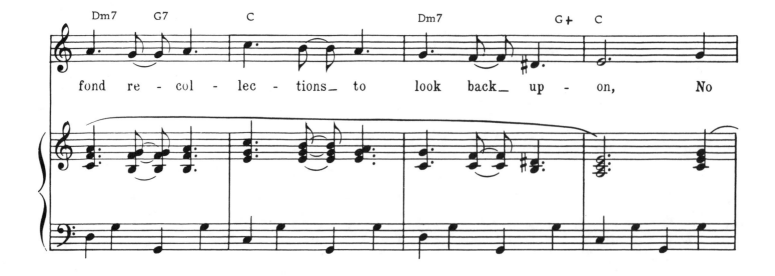

fond re - col - lec - tions_ to look back_ up - on, No

YOU ARE NEVER AWAY

from ALLEGRO (1947)

Lyrics by OSCAR HAMMERSTEIN II
Music by RICHARD RODGERS

163

A COCK-EYED OPTIMIST

from SOUTH PACIFIC (1949)

Lyrics by OSCAR HAMMERSTEIN II
Music by RICHARD RODGERS

HAPPY TALK

from SOUTH PACIFIC (1949)

Lyrics by OSCAR HAMMERSTEIN II
Music by RICHARD RODGERS

172

THERE IS NOTHIN' LIKE A DAME

from SOUTH PACIFIC (1949)

Lyrics by OSCAR HAMMERSTEIN II
Music by RICHARD RODGERS

THIS NEARLY WAS MINE

from SOUTH PACIFIC (1949)

Lyrics by OSCAR HAMMERSTEIN II
Music by RICHARD RODGERS

182

Lyrics: On - ly to fly a - way, On - ly to fly as day flies from moon - light. Now, now I'm a - lone, Still dream-ing of par - a - dise,

184

YOU'VE GOT TO BE CAREFULLY TAUGHT

from SOUTH PACIFIC (1949)

Lyrics by OSCAR HAMMERSTEIN II
Music by RICHARD RODGERS

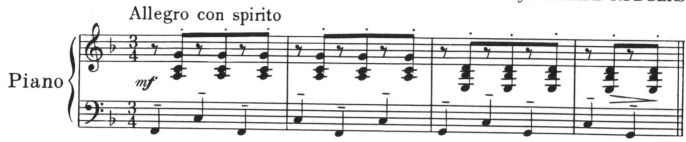

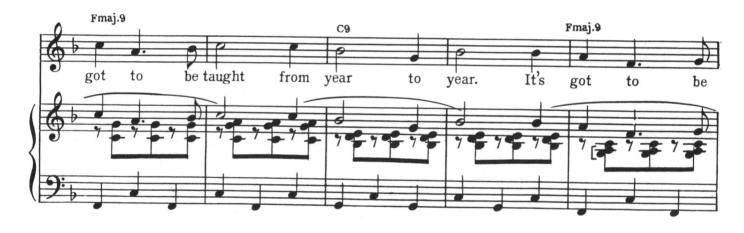

YOUNGER THAN SPRINGTIME

from SOUTH PACIFIC (1949)

Lyrics by OSCAR HAMMERSTEIN II
Music by RICHARD RODGERS

BEAT OUT DAT RHYTHM ON A DRUM

from CARMEN JONES (1943)

Lyrics by OSCAR HAMMERSTEIN II
Music by GEORGES BIZET

194

GETTING TO KNOW YOU

from THE KING AND I (1951)

Lyrics by OSCAR HAMMERSTEIN II
Music by RICHARD RODGERS

HELLO, YOUNG LOVERS

from THE KING AND I (1951)

Lyrics by OSCAR HAMMERSTEIN II
Music by RICHARD RODGERS

I WHISTLE A HAPPY TUNE

from THE KING AND I (1951)

Lyrics by OSCAR HAMMERSTEIN II
Music by RICHARD RODGERS

Coda

MY LORD AND MASTER

from THE KING AND I (1951)

Lyrics by OSCAR HAMMERSTEIN II
Music by RICHARD RODGERS

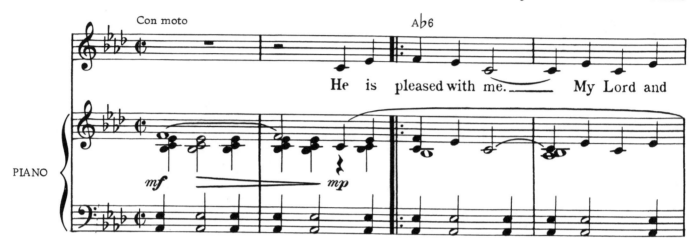

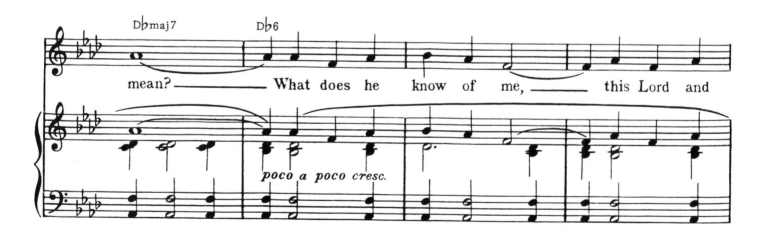

SHALL WE DANCE?

from THE KING AND I (1951)

Lyrics by OSCAR HAMMERSTEIN II
Music by RICHARD RODGERS

man-y men and girls Are in each oth-er's arms, It

made me think we might be sim-i-lar-ly oc-cu-pied.

REFRAIN (Gai ly)

Shall we dance? On a bright cloud of

mu-sic shall we fly? Shall we dance?

218

SOMETHING WONDERFUL

from THE KING AND I (1951)

Lyrics by OSCAR HAMMERSTEIN II
Music by RICHARD RODGERS

THE BIG BLACK GIANT

from ME AND JULIET (1953)

Lyrics by OSCAR HAMMERSTEIN II
Music by RICHARD RODGERS

228

A VERY SPECIAL DAY

from ME AND JULIET (1953)

Lyrics by OSCAR HAMMERSTEIN II
Music by RICHARD RODGERS

232

EVERYBODY'S GOT A HOME BUT ME

from PIPE DREAM (1955)

Lyrics by OSCAR HAMMERSTEIN II
Music by RICHARD RODGERS

236

THE MAN I USED TO BE
from PIPE DREAM (1955)

Lyrics by OSCAR HAMMERSTEIN II
Music by RICHARD RODGERS

THE NEXT TIME IT HAPPENS

from PIPE DREAM (1955)

Lyrics by OSCAR HAMMERSTEIN II
Music by RICHARD RODGERS

243

IN MY OWN LITTLE CORNER

from CINERELLA (1957, television)

Lyrics by OSCAR HAMMERSTEIN II
Music by RICHARD RODGERS

TEN MINUTES AGO

from CINDERELLA (1957, television)

Lyrics by OSCAR HAMMERSTEIN II
Music by RICHARD RODGERS

A HUNDRED MILLION MIRACLES

from FLOWER DRUM SONG (1958)

Lyrics by OSCAR HAMMERSTEIN II
Music by RICHARD RODGERS

258

Coda (*Slowly and tenderly*)

hun - dred mil - lion mir - a - cles are happ - 'ning ev - 'ry

(*Uke tacet*) MEI LI:

day! _____ My fa - ther says the sun will keep ris - ing

(*Uke tacet*)

o - ver the east - ern hill. My fa - ther says he does - n't know why but

OTHERS: It will! ___ some - how or oth - er it will. ___

some - how or oth - er it will. ___

LOVE, LOOK AWAY

from FLOWER DRUM SONG (1958)

Lyrics by OSCAR HAMMERSTEIN II
Music by RICHARD RODGERS

Know-ing I need one man a-lone, And know-ing I have no chance.____

REFRAIN

Moderato espressivo

Love, look a - way!____ Love, look a - way from

me. Fly, when you pass my door, Fly and get lost at

sea. Call it a day.____ Love, let us say we're

YOU ARE BEAUTIFUL

from FLOWER DRUM SONG (1958)

Lyrics by OSCAR HAMMERSTEIN II
Music by RICHARD RODGERS

CLIMB EV'RY MOUNTAIN

from THE SOUND OF MUSIC (1959)

Lyrics by OSCAR HAMMERSTEIN II
Music by RICHARD RODGERS

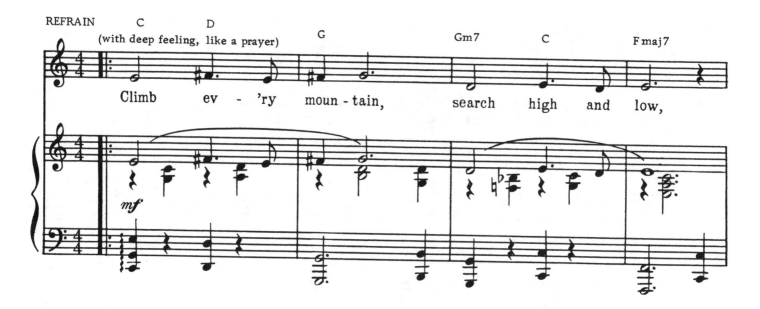

MY FAVORITE THINGS

from THE SOUND OF MUSIC (1959)

Lyrics by OSCAR HAMMERSTEIN II
Music by RICHARD RODGERS

274

EDELWEISS

from THE SOUND OF MUSIC (1959)

Lyrics by OSCAR HAMMERSTEIN II
Music by RICHARD RODGERS

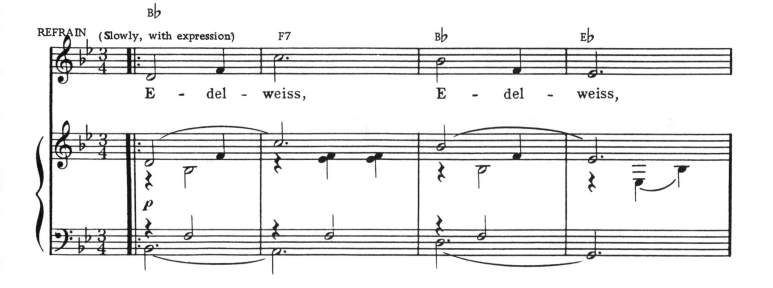

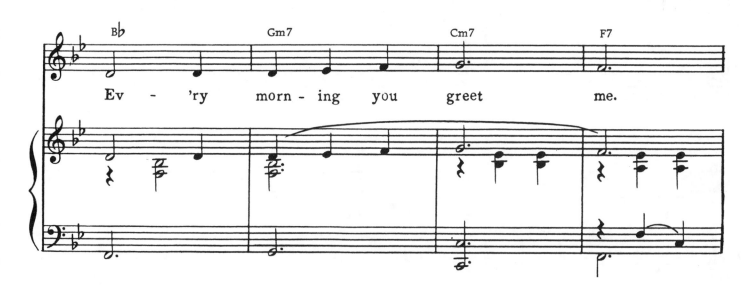

The Rodgers & Hammerstein Collection

BOXED SET

This fabulous gift box is the ultimate collection for anyone who loves the music of Rodgers & Hammerstein. It features nine books for a total of 90 classic songs arranged for piano and voice with guitar chord frames. All the books are packaged in a deluxe hard case for permanent storage and display.

INCLUDES:

CAROUSEL

CINDERELLA

FLOWER DRUM SONG

THE KING AND I

OKLAHOMA!

THE SOUND OF MUSIC

SOUTH PACIFIC

STATE FAIR

It also includes the book **Rodgers & Hammerstein Rediscovered,** a compilation of rare favorites.

■ 00312509/**$59.95**

The Richard Rodgers Collection

Richard Rodgers' contributions to the musical theatre are extraordinary. His career spanned more than 6 decades, and his hits ranged from the silver screens of Hollywood to the bright lights of Broadway. He was the recipient of countless awards, including Pulitzers, Tonys, Oscars, Emmys, and Grammys. He wrote more than 900 published songs and forty Broadway musicals.

This collection features a preface by his widow, Dorothy Rodgers, an introduction by Stephen Holden and a biography by Bert Fink, and 62 of his classic songs complete with the years and the show which produced it. Features such favorites as: **Bali Ha'i • Bewitched • Climb Ev'ry Mountain • Do I Hear A Waltz? • Edelweiss • Getting To Know You • Hello, Young Lovers • I'm Gonna Wash That Man Right Outa My Hair • If I Loved You • Isn't It Romantic • It Might As Well Be Spring • The Lady Is A Tramp • My Favorite Things • My Funny Valentine • Oh, What A Beautiful Mornin' • Some Enchanted Evening • The Sound Of Music • The Surrey With The Fringe On Top • There's A Small Hotel • You Took Advantage Of Me • You'll Never Walk Alone • Younger Than Springtime •** and many more. All songs are arranged for piano and voice with guitar chord frames

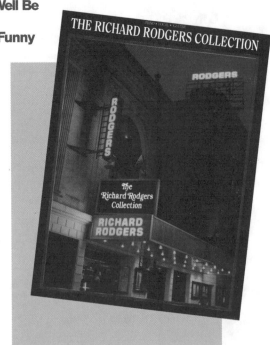

■ 00490422/**$19.95**

FOR MORE INFORMATION, SEE YOUR LOCAL MUSIC DEALER,
OR WRITE TO:

HAL•LEONARD™
C O R P O R A T I O N
7777 W. BLUEMOUND RD. P.O. BOX 13819 MILWAUKEE, WI 53213